The Little Book of Persona Dolls

Using dolls to help children understand the views and feelings of others

Written by
Marilyn Bowles

Illustrations by Martha Hardy

Little Books with **BIG** ideas®

The Little Book of Persona Dolls
ISBN 1 904187 86 2

©Featherstone Education Ltd, 2004
Text ©Marilyn Bowles, 2004
Illustrations ©Martha Hardy, 2004
Series Editor, Sally Featherstone

First published in the UK, January 2004

'Little Books' is a trade mark of Featherstone Education Ltd

Published in the United Kingdom by
Featherstone Education Ltd
44 - 46 High Street
Husbands Bosworth
Leicestershire
LE17 6LP

Printed in the UK on paper produced in the European Union from managed, sustainable forests

Contents

Using persona dolls with young children
Introduction

We live in a big world, with lots of different people!

- ? How can we help children to appreciate the pleasures and meet the challenges of everyday life at home and in our settings?
- ? How can we help them to find out about other people, make friendships and build bridges?
- ? How can we encourage the children we work with to interact with confidence and understanding with the wide variety of people they will meet?
- ? How can we support children as they develop skills of problem solving and emotional intelligence?

This book reflects the practice of authors and educators who work with and write about using dolls to address a range of issues which concern young children.

All manner of issues can be discussed using the dolls. Events and happenings in the dolls' lives are shared with the children and

gradually ways are evolved by the children for coping with bullying, name-calling, unkindness, misunderstanding, gender-bias and different life stances.

By using dolls we can challenge stereotypical opinions, try to understand different feelings and open our children's minds (and our own) to the differences and similarities which make up our global communities.

It is known that children DO begin to discriminate from as early as 2 years old, influenced by the attitudes they see and hear around them. The research quoted by Louise Derman Sparks;

Anti-bias Curriculum: Tools for Empowering Young Children (Washington DC) confirms this.

Why persona dolls?

The purpose of the work with persona dolls is to encourage the children to have some understanding of the lives and feelings of others, and to prevent the stereotyping which can be associated with racism, bigotry and misunderstanding.

Children are naturally very creative and can readily step into imaginary worlds. Using dolls to represent different characters is an easily adopted strategy and prevents putting actual children on the spot.

Using persona dolls in our settings is one way of bringing into the children's reach ideas and issues which they can listen to, become involved in and empathise with.
We can use dolls and their stories to:

* **help children anticipate and prepare for new learning experiences,** by hearing a story of a doll going through a similar experience (a new topic for learning, a school trip or visit, visitors, a new activity, class or teacher);

* **help children understand and deal with their own daily fears, anxieties, pleasures, disappointments,** by listening to stories where the central character (the doll) is experiencing a similar situation (such as anger at having their brick construction knocked over or their new hairstyle ridiculed, the disappointment of a cancelled treat, apprehension before visits to the dentist, parties, injections, dogs, birthdays, being lonely, the dark, spiders);

* **help children understand new situations, feelings, family events, lifestyles, significant happenings,** by brainstorming the range of feelings involved, and talking about options (a new baby in their family, a new child in the class, meeting a child who is adopted, living in a single parent family, new arrivals from another country or culture);

*   **help children challenge unfairness, bias and discrimination** in themselves and others, based on ignorance or lack of experience (teasing, bullying, racial or social name calling, stereotyping by race, language, gender, faith or family circumstances)

What do persona dolls look like?

Any doll can be a persona doll. Some dolls are specially made to reflect different cultures and abilities, but any doll can actually be a persona doll. We would encourage you to look carefully at the dolls you choose, to ensure a variety of facial characteristics, skin colour and body shape/size. (Some manufacturers merely change the colour of the plastic to indicate a change of race!)

Just like the children in your setting, each doll needs a persona (a character, a family, a lifestyle or life stance, likes, dislikes, wishes, hopes and dreams). You will need to create this persona as you introduce the doll to the children.

You will need some dolls who are like the children in your group, and some who are different, so you can relate the events you describe to the children you work with.

Of course, the personas of the dolls will develop over time, and you can always add a new doll to meet a new circumstance or event.

The purpose of the persona is to get the children thinking about people's feelings and to prevent them from forming discriminatory opinions based on ignorance or lack of experience.

Are they different from the dolls in the home corner?

Persona dolls are usually kept in a special place in the setting or class-room. They often sit on a special shelf or vantage point, so they can 'see' what is going on in your setting. They are not usually played with by the children, except during doll story sessions, group times or circle times, although they may accompany a child during a difficult time, or at their special request.

In this way, you can introduce the dolls naturally into events and discussions about everyday successes and achievements of your setting, as well as the difficulties and problems.

Some children will make a special relation-ship with a particular doll, through a story which mirrors their own experiences, or a link through their home or family circumstances. In this case, the child may ask to talk to this special doll at other times. You must use your own discretion to decide how you use the dolls with your group.

You may also want to discuss and decide as a staff group, how the dolls will be used in your setting, so there is a consistent practice in all groups.

How do I start working with dolls?

We would advise you to start by introducing one or two dolls to the children in your setting. The simple steps on the following pages may help you to decide where to start, and how to make persona doll stories part of your setting.

Five steps to successful doll work

Step 1- look at the children in your group, class, or school

Think about the children in your group and ask yourself:
* what is the range of names in the group?
* what races and ethnic groups do the children represent?
* what are their physical appearances and characteristics?
* what are their favourite activities and foods?
* what are their common behaviours?
* what are their family structures and economic classes, parents' occupations and backgrounds, family backgrounds?
* where do they live? What sort of houses and homes?
* what are their religions, languages, cultures, festivals, special days and other celebrations?

Step 2 - now look at the gaps and missing features

Are there any features of our diverse society which are missing from your group?:
* you may not have ethnic diversity
* you may not have a range of family circumstances
* all your children may live in the country or in flats or in inner city terraces
* you may have no children with physical differences, for instance, children with very curly hair or green eyes

Consider these missing features as you build up your collection. Make sure your dolls truly represent not only your class and community, but the whole range of cultures in our country.

Step 3 - find your doll

Find, buy or borrow a doll which you can keep for use as your first persona doll. The doll should be new to the group of children you will introduce it to. For this first doll, try to mirror some of the children in your group, but not one individual. It might be a good idea to choose a boy doll as the first doll – this will help to ensure that the boys in your group are engaged.

Step 4 - talk to the other adults about the first doll

As a staff, discuss the issues you most want to address with the children, and create a simple persona to suit your first doll.

Now discuss which issues you could approach and address with the first doll. You may want to include personal, social or emotional concerns or perhaps an opportunity to explore a faith, a culture or a particular family grouping.

Trisha Whitney in her book 'Kids Like Us' suggests the following guidelines for constructing personas:

* **Balance the characteristics,** including some that are represented in your group, and some that are not.
* **Avoid reinforcing stereotypes** - dolls with disabilities can come from wealthy families, not all black boys live on housing estates, many Asian families prefer European food, not all mums stay at home to look after the kids!
* **Always include some characteristics that your group can share and understand.** Don't make the new character so different that they can't relate to it at all!
* **If the doll is going to share a characteristic** or a home lifestyle very like one of your children, make sure they are very different from them in other ways. Different gender, different race, different family etc.

Decide these things before you give your doll a name.

Health warning!

Don't try to cover too many issues in each doll's persona. If you do, it will be difficult to remember the details and the doll will cease to be a credible character!

The sample dolls in this book will give you some starter ideas, but they are not templates. Use your own knowledge of the children you work with to construct your own characters.

Step 5 - start to record the details of the dolls. This is a very important stage!

You may think this is a very formal approach, but it is absolutely essential to be consistent with each doll, and if you collect several, it's easy to forget which one has which persona! It is also important if the dolls are to be used by different adults and groups of children.

You could record these details in a Persona Doll log or in separate books belonging to each doll. It is important to keep these safe, or make a copy in case you lose the original.

The doll record should contain the following information:

About the doll:
- name
- age
- gender
- colour of hair, eyes, skin
- race or ethnicity
- physical appearance
- likes and dislikes such as favourite food and activities
- disabilities or learning difficulties

About their family and life:
- family structure including siblings and other relatives
- parents' occupations
- where they live
- language, history, culture, religion
- favourite family activities
- festivals and special occasions

Start simple! Even if you have decided on a range of details about the doll, choose just a few to use when you first introduce the doll.
Keep recording! As you use the doll, more details will emerge. You may decide to use two dolls in a story. You

might introduce a new feature into a doll's life - for example, to help a child through a separation, an illness, new glasses, moving house. In this case, you need to write down the new features and influences in the doll's own book or in your Persona Doll log.

Step 6 - introducing the doll to your group

Introductions are sensitive occasions. Plan your introduction carefully. Think about:

* ❋   the **size of the group** (the younger the children, the smaller the group should be);
* ❋   the **location** (the children will need to be somewhere quiet and comfortable);
* ❋   the **length of the session** (aim for a **maximum of 15 minutes**, less if the children are very young);
* ❋   the **format** of the session.

Here is one way you might start:

1.   Use a time and place where you can be quiet with a group of children. Sit in a circle, making sure everyone is comfortable, can hear and can see.

2.   Introduce the doll by naming him/her, and giving a few facts about their character and circumstances (their persona).

3.   Pass the doll round the group, making sure everyone has a turn to greet and hold it.

4.   Establish that the doll is a friend – perhaps one of the children would like to hold them while you discuss something.

5.   Now introduce a "happening' – something happy or sad or difficult that the doll is having to deal with.

Use the notes you have made, and make up a story or situation which the children will recognise:
* *   use familiar places in your setting or community
* *   use language the children will understand

The Little Book of Persona Dolls   **11**

* talk about familiar situations and activities
* try to balance situations within the setting, in the community and at home.

Take care that:
* no children from your setting are named or identified.
* the situation is described in a neutral way (look at the examples in the second part of this book).

Make sure that happy things happen to the doll with which the children can readily identify e.g. going to MacDonald's or having a birthday party.

6. Ask the children to think about how the doll might feel about this situation. Let them talk to someone next to them about this before you ask for suggestions from the group. Use open questions and accept a range of responses - don't just ask one child. You could ask:
    * how do you think he/she felt?
    * what do you think she/he wanted to do?
    * what could she/he do?
    * who could he/she talk to about it?

Try to respond with neutral comments such as:
* That's one way she/he could be feeling. Can anyone think of another way she/he might be feeling?
* That's one thing she/he could do. Can you think of another thing?

Allow them plenty of time to think about their responses – don't be tempted to rush in too soon. Like us, they will need time to think through their ideas, especially about something they haven't experienced for themselves.

Give as many children as possible a chance to speak. Often they will repeat what has gone before, but just as often they have their own special insights.

Finish on a positive note, with one of the good ideas for resolving the issues, so that the children have a guide to what they might do should they be in a similar situation.

The Little Book of Persona Dolls

Don't go on too long. A couple of short sessions work much better than one long one.

Put the doll somewhere where the children can see it and it can 'see' them.

As soon as you can, **write a few notes** so you can remember what has been discussed and whether any further parts of the persona have been added.

You could bring the doll to another session within a couple of days, to remind the children about the doll and to and include the doll in your work.

Links with the Early Learning Goals and Foundation Profile

As you work with persona dolls, you will realise their enormous potential to help children develop in all sorts of ways. Practitioners will also want to know the detail of how and where they fit in the curriculum for personal, social and emotional development in the Foundation Stage.

The following goals are particularly relevant to the work in this book:

SD7   Understand that people have different needs, views, cultures and beliefs that need to be treated with respect;

SD8   Understand that s/he can expect others to treat her or his needs, views, cultures, and beliefs with respect;

ED6   Have a developing respect for own culture and beliefs and those of other people;

ED7   Consider the consequences of words & actions for self & others

LCT7   Use talk to organise, sequence & clarify thinking, ideas feelings and events, exploring the meanings and sounds of new words;

KUW6   Find out about past & present events in own life, & in those of family members & other people s/he knows. Begins to know about own cultures and beliefs & those of other people.

...and finally

Remember:

Each doll's persona is one of many and as with 'real' people they are all different.

Each persona represents ONE way of being Sikh or wheel-chair dependent or scare or fostered, and this needs to be emphasised regularly to prevent stereotyping.

The following pages describe a range of persona dolls, each experiencing a different life style, with its attendant difficulties and delights. Please use them as models for your own work, but remember, your setting is unique, the children you work with are unique and the situations you experience together are unique to you. So adapt, reorganise change or add to the characters we offer you.

Always select dolls and situations with care, and make sure that the work you do is sensitively matched to your children's needs.

Your journey with persona dolls begins with
just one step.....so now,
let's get going!

Part 2 - Some dolls and their personas

The dolls on the following pages are examples of persona dolls which have already been used in Foundation Stage and key Stage One groups. They are included here to help you begin or extend your work with persona dolls.

Each doll is introduced, and their persona is briefly described. Family members and family life are outlined, including some details of race, religion, family structure and home life.

On the two pages which follow the introduction of the doll, we have included:

* a few of the objects you would find if you visited the character at home. Some of these objects are of cultural or religious significance, many are not. They are included to make each persona more rounded.

* a simple activity which the doll character enjoys, so your children can share a real experience with them.

* three sets of discussion points and questions which you could use with children of different ages and experience. We do not suggest that you use all the discussion points and questions, certainly not during one session! They are ideas and starters. Pick one or two if you wish, or make up your own from the experiences of your group.

Introducing
Dawn

Dawn's persona

* Dawn is nearly five. She has straight blonde hair and blue eyes.
* Dawn has just started school.
* She has a mum and a dad and her mum is going to have a baby in three weeks time. Her dad works in an office every day. he goes to work on the train and gets back just as Dawn is going to bed. Sometimes he reads her a story before he has his tea.
* Dawn's favourite food is fish fingers and chips, with ketchup. She also likes bananas and apples.

What Dawn likes, thinks and believes

* Dawn loves playing with her toys and games in her bedroom. She makes a house by putting her duvet over two chairs, and crawling underneath with her teddies and dolls.
* Dawn used to go to nursery school, but she has stopped going while her mum is pregnant, to keep her company.
* In the afternoon, they sit on the settee and read books or watch the TV or videos. Dawn really likes being with her mum.
* Sometimes Dawn helps her mum with the shopping. She gets things from the shelves and helps to push the trolley because her mum gets very tired. Last time they went shopping, they went to the baby shop and got a car seat for the new baby.

The best days of Dawn's year are:
* The summer when they go on holiday to Spain.
* Christmas when her best auntie comes to stay.
* Sundays, when Dawn and her dad make her mum breakfast in bed.

What Dawn wishes

❂ Dawn wishes she could stay at home with her mum every day. She doesn't like school very much.

❂ She wishes she could have a black kitten.

❂ Dawn hopes that her mum will still love her when the baby comes. Sometimes she has bad dreams and she thinks her mum is going to forget to come and fetch her from school.

Some things you will find in Dawn's home

* Lots of toys and dolls in a big basket in the living room.
* Lots of baby things ready for the baby.
* A suitcase ready packed for when Dawn's mum goes to the hospital to have the baby.
* Baby magazines, catalogues and books of names.
* A computer that Dawn's dad uses for his work. Sometimes he lets Dawn have a go, but it doesn't have games on like the one at school.
* A big comfy settee with lots of cushions.
* Photos in silver frames of Dawn with her mum and dad.
* A gold clock on the mantelpiece. You can see the insides of the clock going round, and it chimes every hour.

Sometimes Dawn makes paper babies with her mum. This is how you do it.

What you need:
  * a strip of paper about 30cm long and 12cm wide
  * pens or crayons
  * scissors

What you do:
1. Fold the paper into a zig-zag with 8 folds. This will make four babies.
2. Draw the outline of half a sitting-down baby on the top fold of the paper. Make sure the middle of the baby comes on the fold and the arms and legs come to the edge of the paper so the babies join hands in a row.
3. Cut through all the layers of paper, round the baby outline, taking care that the hands and feet are still joined.
4. Unfold the babies, draw faces and hair, colour their clothes - make them all the same or all different. You could even make twins or quads!

The Little Book of Persona Dolls

Some talking points for younger children

? Do your mum and dad have to go to work? How do you feel about that? Do they come home late?

? Dawn's mum gets very tired. What could Dawn do to help her? What do you do to help your mum?

? Have you got a computer at home? Do you have a go on it sometimes?

Some talking points for older children

? Dawn's mum is having a new baby soon. What can you tell Dawn about babies?

? A boy told Dawn she was a cry baby. What would you say to him if you heard him say that?

? Dawn doesn't like coming to school much. She misses her mum. How could you help her? What could you do or say?

? Have you got a favourite auntie or uncle? What are they like? What do they do? When do you see them?

? One day, Dawn's mum went to sleep on the settee and didn't come to meet her from school. She didn't forget, she was just so tired! How do you think Dawn felt?
Mrs Saunders phoned and woke Dawn's mum up. She waited with Dawn till her mum came. Dawn's mum was really out of breath when she got to school. How do you think she felt? How did Dawn feel when she saw her mum coming up the path?

and for the philosophers in your setting!

? Dawn's mum and dad will be very busy when the new baby comes. There is such a lot to do. How can they make sure Dawn doesn't feel left out? What can Dawn do to help?

Introducing
William

William's persona

* William is five years old. He has brown hair and blue eyes.
* He wears glasses to help his eyes.
* William doesn't have any brothers or sisters and he is sometimes a bit lonely at home. He's a bit shy at school too.
* His Mum and Dad talk a lot and they all have great conversations altogether.
* William's mum and dad go to car boot sales to raise money for 'Jump Rope for Heart'. William goes too.

What William likes, thinks and believes

* William believes that every one should help each other and not be unkind or bully people.
* He loves animals and likes to watch wild life programmes on the TV.
* When he's a bit bigger and can write really well he's going to write to the local paper to tell them about Jump Rope for Heart (he has already had his photo in the paper once).
* His Dad likes gardening and has an allotment too – they eat lots of fresh vegetables for dinner. William likes carrots best.
* William's mum and dad believe that everyone should try to make the world a better place for everyone.

The best days of William's year are:
* Jump Rope for Heart Day when he skips to raise money for heart research.
* Going to Flower and Vegetable Shows with his Mum and Dad. Sometimes his dad and mum win a prize for the best vegetables, fruit or flowers. Once, William won a prize for a miniature garden he made on a plate. That really was a great day!

What William wishes

✪ William would like to have a best friend. What could he do to make friends?

✪ William would love to have a pet. His mum says they are a lot of work.

✪ William would like everyone to be kind and not tease other people.

Some things you will find in William's home

* A green box for recycling tins, paper and cardboard
* A compost bin in a corner of his garden
* Lots of picture books about animals
* Lots of gardening magazines and books
* All sorts of vegetables in the kitchen and in the freezer
* A cupboard under the stairs, with lots of things saved up for his next sale – old toys, comics, ornaments
* A magnifying glass for when he is looking at little pictures and writing
* A skipping rope – he's practising for the next 'Jump Rope for Heart' event

William's favourite skipping rhymes to learn and play:

'Charlie Chaplin washing up,
Broke a saucer and a cup.
How much did they cost?
1p, 2p, 3p ....'

(go on as long as you can - how far can you count?)

'Chocolate cake, when you bake,
How many minutes do you take?
1 minute, 2 minutes, 3 minutes......'

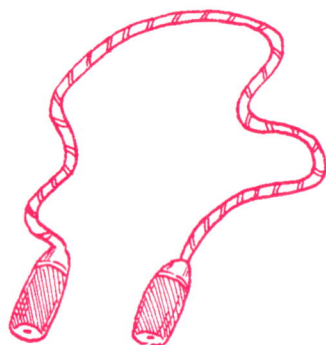

Some talking points for younger children

? At William's school if anyone is unkind they get into trouble. What happens here if someone is being unkind?

? Have you ever put some money in a charity box and got a sticker or a poppy? What is the money for?

? Have you ever won a prize? How did you feel?

Some talking points for older children

? William doesn't like wearing glasses but he can't see well without them. How do you think he feels about that?

? Sometimes unkind children laugh at him and even call him names. Why do you think they do that? What could William do about it?

? When William is in the playground he has to be careful not to bump into other people when they are playing. How do you think the other children could help him?

? William is very shy, but he will talk in assembly if he's explaining about one of his fund-raising stalls! Are you brave enough to speak in assembly?

? At William's school if anyone is unkind they get into trouble. What happens here if someone is being unkind? What can you do if you are bullied?

and for the real philosophers in your setting!

? When William collects things to sell at the car boot sales, he really enjoys himself. Is there anything you do for other people that you really enjoy?

Introducing
Geeta

Geeta's persona

* Geeta is a five year old girl . She has brown skin, straight black hair and brown eyes.
* She has a big brother called Prakash who is eight, and a Mum and Dad who work in a factory making tee shirts, sweatshirts and sweaters.
* Geeta has always lived in a little house in a big city.
* She is a Hindu and her family follow her religion closely.
* Her favourite foods are Macdonald's fries and samosas.

What Geeta likes, thinks and believes

* Geeta loves dressing up at school. She always dresses up as the mum in the home corner, and cooks pretend food for the other children.
* In Geeta's home there is a shrine where the family say prayers every day.
* The whole family go to the mandir (religious meeting place) several times a week to offer gifts of food and money, and to pray.
* Geeta and Prakash her brother go to the mandir on Fridays after school to learn their mother tongue which is Gujurati.
* Geeta's family are vegetarian. This means they don't eat meat.

The best days of Geeta's year are:
* The festival of Holi, which is in the spring.
* The Raksha Bandhan ritual in the summer when Prakash gives her a woven bracelet.
* Navratri, which is 10 nights of dancing parties in the autumn.
* And Divali, the autumn festival of light before the Hindu New Year.

What Geeta wishes

✿ Geeta wishes she could bring some of her favourite samosas to school to share with her friends.

✿ Geeta wishes her mum and dad didn't have to go to work. She came first in a race on Sports Day and they couldn't come because they were at work. How do you think she felt?

✿ Geeta wishes she could go to the country, where it's peaceful and quiet.

Some things you will find in Geeta's home

* A roti board and roller which Geeta's Mum uses every day to make fresh roti (chappatti – like a pancake).
* Large saucepans for cooking rice, curries and vegetables.
* A shrine to Ganesh, the elephant god, with flowers, small candles called divas and little statues of Ganesh, which they wash and dress each day as part of their worship.
* Pictures on the walls of their special god, Ganesh.
* A TV with BBC, ITV and Asian channels with news, films and Asian music.
* Geeta's mum wears lots of of gold jewellery and coloured bangles. She is always taking them off and leaving them everywhere!

Geeta likes making Mehndi patterns with her mum

Asian people make beautiful mehndi patterns on their hands for weddings and other parties.*(You may want to inform parents about this before you start, so they know what their child is doing and why)*

What you need:
* special Mehndi paint (you can buy this in ready made 'icing bags') or make your own by mixing henna dye and water to a thick paste, and putting it in a plastic bag.
* clean hands or feet (or both)

What you do:
1. Snip off the pointed end or corner of the bag.
2. Gently squeeze the bag so the henna paint comes out. Make swirly or flower patterns on your hand or foot.
3. Leave to dry for about an hour (if you can wait that long!).
4. Gently wash off the henna to show a pattern which lasts a few days.

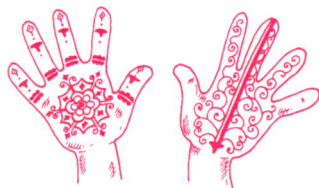

The Little Book of Persona Dolls

Some talking points for younger children

? Do your mum and dad have to go to work? How do you feel about that? Why do they have to go?

? Geeta's mum wears a sari. Have you seen anyone wearing a sari? Have you ever tried a sari on?

? Have you ever tried Asian (Indian) food? Did you like it? What is your favourite food?

Some talking points for older children

? Geeta's best friend said her favourite dinner looked disgusting because it has lots of food in it that he'd never seen before. How do you think Geeta felt?

? Geeta's brother was very upset when some big boys called him 'Paki'. Who could he tell? What could he do?

? Geeta and Prakash can speak two languages. Can you speak more than one language?

? Geeta has brown skin. What it is like to have dark brown skin?

? Geeta's favourite festival is Divali. At Divali the family celebrate with their whole family. They have lots of good food, new clothes, presents and gifts of money. When does your family celebrate?

and for the philosophers in your setting!

? How do you think Geeta feels when she worships in the mandir? How and where can we find out about the mandir?

Introducing
Ross

Ross's persona

*   Ross is a five year old African-Caribbean boy. He was born in London and has not been to Africa or the Caribbean but he would love to go!
*   He has black, very curly hair, brown eyes and dark brown skin.
*   He has an older sister called Channelle and his best friend is called John.
*   He really likes dancing and singing – he dances everywhere!
*   Ross loves to eat spicy rice and peas that his Gran makes.

What Ross likes, thinks and believes

* Ross's Gran is a Christian and she takes Ross and Channelle to Church with her every Sunday where they sing lots of songs, clap and shout, and there's loud music; his Mum and Dad just go on special occasions.
* His Gran believes in God and Jesus and the Holy Spirit. Ross loves his Gran and wants to believe what she believes but his Mum and Dad aren't sure – so he's not sure either.
* His Gran has taught him how to sing lots of songs.
* Ross loves music time at school. He joins in every song and sings VERY loudly!

The best days of Ross's year are:
  * Martin Luther King Day in January (his Mum and Dad come to this).
  * Easter and Christmas at his Gran's church, celebrated with lots of food and music.
  * The Carnival parade in the city, when Ross watches and blows his Carnival whistle.

What Ross wishes

❁ Ross wishes his friend John would always play with him and not the other boys and girls.

❁ Ross wishes it was music time all day at school!

❁ Ross wishes he could go to Africa and go on safari to see lions and elephants.

Some things you will find in Ross's home

* Ross has lots of clothes and his mum is always washing and ironing them and making him hang them up to keep them smart.
* He has lots of story books. His favourite is about Anansi the spider man, who is a special character from the Caribbean: he's very crafty and play tricks on people.
* Brushes and combs so his sister Channelle can have her hair done in tiny plaits called canerow.
* At the weekend, you will see Caribbean food – Ross's favourite rice and peas, sweet potatoes, sugar cane and mango or jerk chicken.
* Whistles on ribbons, which the children use when it is carnival (and when they are feeling very noisy!).

Ross loves singing songs with his Gran. Here are the words of one of his favourites.

Wide, wide is the ocean
High as the heavens above,
Deep, deep as the deepest sea
Is my Saviour's love.
I though so unworthy.
Still am a child of his care,
For his word teaches me and his love reaches me
EVERYWHERE

The Little Book of Persona Dolls

Some talking points for younger children

? Do you get cross with your friends sometimes? How do you make friends again?

? If you could go anywhere, where would you choose to go? What would you do there?

? Have you got a Grandma? Does she come and see you?

Some talking points for older children

? When Ross's Gran comes to collect him from school she is very loud and sometimes sings loud songs and every body looks. Why do you think Ross is embarrassed? What could he do about that?

? When John comes to tea, sometimes he doesn't like the food that Ross likes – what should Ross do or say?

? Sometimes Ross wishes his hair was like John's and he could make it look like Beckham's latest style, but it is very tight and curly. What can you say to Ross, so that he is happy about his hair? Is there anything you wish was different about the way you are? Why?

? When it is music or dancing time, everybody wants to watch Ross dance, because he is very good. How do you think he feels when everyone is looking at him? What are you good at? Can you show other people too?

and for the philosophers in your setting!

? Once he was playing with John, and John wanted to be the doctor as well and told Ross to 'Go back to your own country'. Ross was very upset because he's IN his own country. What could he do to sort this out?

Introducing
Phoebe

Phoebe's persona

*   Phoebe has brown wavy hair, white skin and blue eyes.
*   She is four years old and she has a big brother called Paul. He is eleven.
*   She lives with her Mum, but her Dad lives somewhere else.
*   Phoebe sees her Dad every Saturday and they go to the park, to the cinema or to MacDonald's.
*   Phoebe likes going to school but she is sometimes a bit shy.
*   Her favourite food is cheese sandwiches.

What Phoebe likes, thinks and believes

* Phoebe likes doing quiet things like puzzles, listening to taped stories and playing with the Playmobil farm. She loves horses!
* Phoebe is pleased when she looks at all the beautiful animals in the world and when it's a sunny day, so she can play outside.
* She is not happy when people argue and fight, especially her Mum and Dad. She thinks you should say sorry and try to be friends with people, even if you don't like them.
* Her mum and dad say that people should try to work out their problems by talking to each other, and not expecting someone else to sort things out or praying.

The best days of Phoebe's year are:
* Her birthday, when she can have 3 friends round to play games and eat party food.
* Christmas, when they all decorate the house and have a tree with lots of lights and presents.

What Phoebe wishes

❀ Phoebe wishes her mum and dad still lived together.

❀ Phoebe wishes she could have a holiday on a pony farm and ride a real pony.

❀ Phoebe wishes she was brave like her brother Paul. He is in the school band and Phoebe went to watch them play once. Paul even sang a song in front of all those people, and she could hear every word!

Some things you will find in Phoebe's home

* Lots of house plants which she waters for her Mum.
* Jigsaw puzzles and story tapes. She likes the 'Kipper' stories and 'Each Peach Pear Plum' best.
* Barbie wallpaper in Phoebe's bedroom and a pink duvet and a pink carpet.
* A hamster cage – sometimes with a hamster in it!
* A drawing book and felt pens and lots of pictures that Phoebe has already finished colouring. Her mum sticks them on the fridge-freezer.
* Loud music when her brother Paul is at home!
* Paul's football kit, bag and school shoes on the hall floor.
* Baking tins for making cakes with her Mum.

Phoebe's dad likes these chocolate rock cakes, so she sometimes makes them at her dad's flat.

What you need:
* 8 tablespoons plain flour
* 2 teaspoons baking powder
* 2 tablespoons cocoa
* 4 tablespoons margarine
* 3 tablespoons sugar
* Chocolate bits
* 1 egg

What you do:
1. Mix everything together.
2. Spoon small heaps onto a greased baking tray.
3. Cook for 20 minutes at 160 C.
4. Cool on a wire tray before eating!

The Little Book of Persona Dolls

Some talking points for younger children

? When Phoebe gets home from school she likes to relax by doing puzzles. What do you do when you get home?

? Phoebe had a hamster but it was poorly, then it died. How do you think Phoebe felt? What could her Mum do to help her be happy again?

? Sometimes at school Phoebe doesn't have anyone to play with. What could she do to find someone?

Some talking points for older children

? Phoebe wishes that her Dad and Mum were still friends and lived at the same house. Why do you think they don't?

? When she has a birthday she likes to play quiet party games. What games do you like to play at parties? Why?

? Once Phoebe's best friend said Phoebe's Dad didn't love her because he didn't live at their house. How do you think Phoebe felt? What do you think she could do about that?

? Why do people fall out with each other?

? Phoebe wants to write long stories when she is bigger. What do you want to be able to do when you are bigger?

and for the philosophers in your setting!

? Phoebe wishes her Dad would come to see her work at school and talk to her teacher, but he never knows when it's the right day. What could Phoebe do about that?

The Little Book of Persona Dolls

Introducing
Ahmed

Ahmed's persona

* Ahmed has a Mum and Dad, a big brother called Uzair and a baby called Safiyya.
* Ahmed is a Muslim. He has dark brown hair, brown eyes and light brown skin.
* Ahmed goes to school in the daytime, and then to another school in the evening at the Mosque.
* He loves going to the library near his house to look at books.
* His Dad is a builder and Ahmed wants to be one too.

The Little Book of Persona Dolls

What Ahmed likes, thinks and believes

* Ahmed and his family pray to Allah (God).
* Many Muslims pray 5 times day: Ahmed's Dad does this at the Mosque. His Mum prays at home using her prayer mat.
* At the Madrassa (the Mosque school) Ahmed learns to read the Qur'an which is written in Arabic.
* Ahmed loves playing with Lego. He builds houses, factories and bridges. Sometimes in the holidays his dad takes him to his work to watch the builders. He loves that!

The most important days of Ahmed's year are:
* The holy month of Ramadan when grown up Muslim's fast (they eat no food during the day) and pray to be better people.
* At the end of Ramadan, there is a wonderful festival called Eid when Ahmed celebrates by wearing new clothes, giving and getting presents and eating special food with all his family.

NB There are different kinds of Muslims who have different ways of worshipping but they all believe in Allah and his prophet Mohammed (pbuh – Peace Be Upon Him)

What Ahmed wishes

❁ Ahmed wishes he was grown up, so he could help his dad every day.

❁ Ahmed wishes everyone could be friends.

❁ Ahmed wishes he could visit his cousins who live in Manchester. They moved there last year and he really misses them.

Some things you will find in Ahmed's home

* A large toy box with lots of Lego and lots of Lego on the floor!
* TWO new sofas! (blue, with little lines of red on them).
* His Mum's prayer mat and Ahmed's small mat.
* A large pan for frying samosas.
* Plates of dates and a bottle of holy water called zum zum.
* Ahmed's kufni (like a long shirt) and his topi (hat).
* Some Arabic writing on the wall near the door. This is a special prayer that the family say every time they go out
* A special place where a covered copy of the Qur'an is kept: this is the family's special holy book.

Ahmed is beginning to learn how to write in Arabic. Here is some Arabic writing that his brother Uzair did for him to copy.

You could try copying or tracing it.

ح خ ج ش ث ت ب ا

خ د ذ ر ز س

ش ص ض ط ظ ع

غ ن ت ك ل م

Some talking points for younger children

? Do your mum and dad have to go to work? How do you feel about that? Why do they have to go?

? Ahmed's Dad is building a wall between the adventure playground and his school. How do you think Ahmed feels about that?

? How can we find out what a mosque looks like?

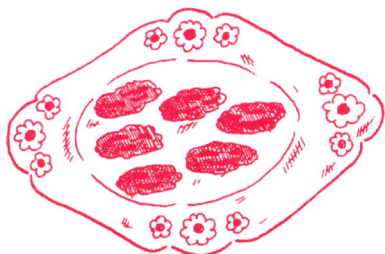

Some talking points for older children

? How do you think Ahmed feels when he goes to work with his Dad?

? Do you think it would be hard to learn the Arabic language? What do you find hard to learn?

? When Ahmed goes to the Madrassa school he wears a special hat called a topi. One day some unkind children took his topi and threw it over a hedge. How do you think Ahmed felt? What do you think he should do if it happens again?

? Ahmed loves the special festival called Eid which comes at the end of Ramadan. Can you think of any other special festivals?

and for the philosophers in your setting!

? Ahmed eats hallal meat, which means it has been prepared in a special way. It is sometimes easier for him to say he is vegetarian when he goes to visit a friend's house. What do you like to eat when you go visiting? Have you ever had something you'd never eaten before?

Introducing
Mei Ling

Mei Ling's persona

* Mei Ling loves going to school. She is six and she has black eyes and straight black hair.
* She can speak two languages: Cantonese and English.
* She laughs a lot because most of the time she is very happy.
* Mei Ling is Chinese and her family have lived in the UK for a long time. Mei Ling can speak more English than her Mum!
* Mei Ling's grandad lives with her and looks after her when her mum and dad work. He doesn't speak English at all.

What Mei Ling likes, thinks and believes

* Mei Ling loves eating noodles. She can use chopsticks.
* Mei Ling loves her family, specially her Grandad.
* Her family tell Mei Ling about great teachers from Chinese history. She tries to remember what they say!
    - Confucius said people should be brave, polite and honest.
    - Laozi said that people should respect nature.
    - Buddha said that people should have a simple life and show kindness to all living things.
* Mei Ling goes to Chinese school on Sunday afternoon.

The best days of Mei Ling's year are:
* Christmas, when her mum and dad have a holiday from work.
* Chinese New Year when her family have lots of special food: sometimes she watches the Lion Dancers on TV.
* A time in the autumn when they eat moon cakes and celebrate the harvest.
* Her birthday when she visits her Chinese friends in Birmingham.

What Mei Ling wishes

⚙ Mei Ling wishes she had a baby brother or sister.

⚙ She would like everyone to enjoy school like she does. Some children don't like going to school.

⚙ She wishes she could visit China and see the cherry blossom. There is a picture of it on her mum's bedroom wall.

⚙ Sometimes Mei Ling is sad when she sees sick animals on the TV.

Some things you will find in Mei Ling's home

* Books, newspapers and pictures with Chinese writing, and Chinese films on videos and DVDs.
* A dragon ornament of green stone – the family like dragons because they are friendly and helpful.
* A panda bear soft toy which her Grandad bought her
* A Chinese calendar with the 12 special animals decorating it. There is a different animal for every year.
* A red paper lantern lamp shade with some Chinese writing which says 'Good Luck'.
* A small family temple where her family pray for their ancestors (grandparents and great-grandparents).
* Chopsticks and little bowls which Mei Ling and her family use for eating Chinese food.

At Chinese school Mei Ling learns to write Chinese characters. You could try Chinese writing too.

Some talking points for younger children

? Have you got a grandad? Does he live near you?

? Mei Ling looks different from everyone else in her class. How do you think she feels about that? What do you think about that?

? Have you ever tried Chinese food? Did you like it? Did you eat with chopsticks?

Some talking points for older children

? Mei Ling goes to a Chinese school every Sunday afternoon to learn how to write Chinese Cantonese letters, but it is very hard work. What do you do that is hard work?

? Mei Ling's Dad works in a Chinese restaurant. Sometimes she hears people call him 'A Chinkie' – how do you think he feels? What should she do when this upsets her?

? Mei Ling's family came from Hong Kong to this country. Can you find where that is in an atlas? Where were you born?

? Her Dad says Chinese people are patient and quiet. Sometimes Mei Ling is impatient. What does that mean? Do you get impatient sometimes?

and for the philosophers in your setting!

? Sometimes Mei Ling's mum can't understand what the teacher is saying and Mei Ling has to explain to her. Are there things about school that you have to explain to your Mum?

Introducing
Tim

Tim's persona

* Tim is five. He has light brown hair and grey eyes. He has a baby sister called Ruth and a Mum and Dad.
* Tim has Down's Syndrome.
* His favourite TV programme is Thomas the Tank engine.
* His favourite food is fish fingers and baked beans.
* He goes to school on a bus which comes to collect him from his house.
* At his school there is a swimming pool AND a ball pool!

What Tim likes, thinks and believes

* Tim likes colouring pictures of dinosaurs. He can write their names when he has his dinosaur book to help him.
* Tim loves singing and dancing. He knows the words to lots of songs and he sings them very loudly!
* Tim loves watching Thomas the Tank Engine on TV and looking at the story books.
* Tim goes to Sunday School on Sunday morning.
* Tim and his family try to be kind to everyone and never tease people.

The best days of Tim's year are:
* Christmas. Last year Tim was a king in the Christmas Nativity Play at school.
* Harvest Festival. He can still remember the smell of all the fruit and vegetables in the church.
* His birthday. Last year he had a card with Thomas on the front, and a badge.

What Tim wishes

⚙ Tim wishes he could go in the Ball Pool at his school every day!

⚙ He wishes he could read the words in his dinosaur book, like his cousin Mark can.

⚙ Tim would like everyone to be kind and stop teasing.

Some things you will find in Tim's home

* Thomas the Tank Engine videos, comics and books.
* A music centre where Tim plays lots of CDs for dancing and singing.
* Tim's and Ruth's toys in big toy boxes.
* A chain on the front door to keep everybody safe.
* A big comfy settee with a snuggly blanket where Tim can rest when he's tired.
* Lots of paper and crayons because Tim loves to draw and colour.
* A gate at the top of the stairs to stop Ruth falling down.

Tim likes making and eating deep sea jelly with fish in!

What you need:
* 1 sachet (1 tbsp) gelatin OR a packet of yellow jelly
* 3 tablespoons hot water   * 600ml (1 pint) clear apple juice
* a few drops of blue and green food colouring
* jelly fish, liquorice strands

What you do:
1.   Put the hot water in the bowl; sprinkle the gelatin on top, or follow the jelly instructions.
2.   Stir until the gelatin has fully melted.
3.   Add the apple juice and a few drops of colouring (a mixture of blue and green will make a suitable colour).
4.   Pour half the jelly into a clear glass or plastic bowl and leave it to set for a while.
5.   When the jelly is beginning to really set, add the jelly fish, and liquorice strands for seaweed. Then add the rest of the jelly.
6.   Leave to set, tip out onto a plate or serve from the mould.

The Little Book of Persona Dolls

Some talking points for younger children

? Tim loves to take his shoes and socks off and bounce on the settee. What do you think his mum says?

? At school Tim finds it hard to do writing. What do you find hard to do at school?

? Tim gets tired very quickly because he has a poorly heart. Do you know any one who is poorly?

Some talking points for older children

? Tim was born with Down's Syndrome. How could we find out more about Down's Syndrome and what it is?

? When Tim is ill he has to stay at home. What will he miss when he doesn't go to school? Why should you go to school every day?

? Tim's best friend Mandy goes to his school. One day she upset him because she said he dribbled. How do you think he felt? What do you think he could do about how he felt?

? Tim is very happy when he is dancing with his friends at the school disco. What makes you really happy in school?

? What things make you sad? What can you do about that?

and for the philosophers in your setting!

? Sometimes when Tim is on the bus going into town with his Mum people stare at him. Why do you think they stare at him? How would you feel if someone stared at you?

Introducing
Elizabeth

Elizabeth's persona

* Elizabeth is nearly six. She has curly brown hair, brown eyes and very dark brown skin. She is in a Reception class in school.
* She lives with her mum and dad in a hostel with lots of other people from different countries. They are asylum seekers.
* Elizabeth comes from Rwanda, a country in Africa.
* Elizabeth couldn't speak any English when she first started at her new school. Now she is learning to speak English well with her friends, but she is sometimes shy with adults.

What Elizabeth likes, thinks and believes

* Elizabeth loves plants and gardening. In Rwanda, she had her own little garden, and she grew tomatoes and sweet corn to eat.
* Her favourite food is sweet corn and mangoes (but not both together!).
* Elizabeth loves books and stories. her mum and dad tell her stories from Africa every night. Her favourite book at school is Handa's Surprise because it reminds her of the animals and fruit of Africa.
* She also likes going shopping with her mum. Elizabeth's family don't have much money to spend, but they do like looking at all the things in the shops.
* Elizabeth would like to find a little house for all her family.

The best days of Elizabeth's year in Africa were:
* A day in the big city a day away from her home.
* Planting the seeds in her garden.
* Picking tomatoes in the garden with her mum.
* Elizabeth really enjoyed the Bonfire Night fireworks this year.

What Elizabeth wishes

❀ Elizabeth wishes that everyone had a home with a garden where they could be safe.

❀ She wishes her family could go back to Rwanda and be safe.

❀ Elizabeth really wants to learn to read in English, so she can read Handa's Surprise to her mum.

Some things you will find in Elizabeth's home

* Elizabeth and her parents live in one room. it has two beds and three chairs.
* There is a big cupboard for all their clothes.
* When Elizabeth came from Rwanda she couldn't bring her toys. Some kind people have given her a doll and some puzzles.
* A photo of Elizabeth's grandad who is still in Africa.
* Magazines from the newsagent next door to their home.
* A mobile phone.

Elizabeth likes making African patterns like the ones on her mum's skirts and dresses.

In Rwanda Elizabeth and her Mum wore a long strip of patterned cloth, sometimes like a skirt, sometimes like a dress. These cloths are brightly coloured, with lovely patterns.

Here is an African pattern for you to look at. Can you copy the patterns? Look carefully at them before you start.

50

Some talking points for younger children

❓ Would you like to live in one room with all your family?

❓ Elizabeth likes shopping with her mum. Where do you like going with your mum or dad?

❓ Have you ever eaten mango or sweet corn? Did you like it?

Some talking points for older children

❓ When Elizabeth first went to her new school, all the other children had pale skins and she was the only one with very dark skin. How do you think she felt? What do you think the other children thought? How could they make her feel welcome?

❓ Elizabeth is learning English and she can say lots of things now. How would you talk to someone if they couldn't understand you?

❓ Elizabeth and her family miss having a garden and growing their own food to eat. What could they do about this?

❓ Elizabeth misses her grandad very much. She looks at his photo every night and says 'Grandad I love you'. Do you have some relatives who are far away? Do you miss them? What do you do to remember them?

❓ Where is Rwanda? Can you find it on a map or globe?

and for the philosophers in your setting!

❓ Elizabeth and her family don't know if they will be able to stay in this country. How do you think they feel about that?

Introducing
Liam

Liam's persona

* Liam is four and a half. He has curly auburn hair and green eyes. He is smaller than most of the other kids in his group.
* Liam really wants to live with his Mum, but she can't look after him at the moment, so he lives with his foster Mum and Dad. They are called Sharon and Jim.
* His favourite foods are Jaffa cakes and crisps.
* At Liam's foster home there is a big garden with a swing.

What Liam likes, thinks and believes

* At his Mum's house Liam jumps on his bed, but Sharon doesn't like him to do it in her house.
* Liam likes Spiderman and Batman movies. he pretends to be Spiderman on the climbing frame at Nursery.
* Liam likes being outside, and he feels great when he's running in the garden or on the grass at the park.
* He loves being on the swing in Sharon and Jim's garden. He can swing so high he can see over the hedge and into the field where the horses live.
* Liam hears stories about God at Nursery school. He says prayers but he's not sure why, because he doesn't always get what he asks for.

The best days of Liam's year are:
* Going to the bonfire night at a city park because he loves loud fireworks.
* The Easter holiday play scheme at church.
* Going to his Gran's house at the seaside in the summer holiday.

What Liam wishes

✪ He wishes that he could be at his mum's all the time even though it is really good fun with his foster family. He would like to have his mum living at Sharon and Jim's house, so they could all be together.

✪ Liam wishes he could fly like Batman. He knows he can't really!

✪ He wishes he could stay outdoors all day until bedtime, or live on a farm with lots of animals.

Some things you will find in Liam's home

* Liam's mum's home is a small flat but it has lots of Liam's toys all over the floor.
* He has a play station in his bedroom and toys on the floor.
* His Mum has lots of pop star pictures all over the walls in her bedroom.
* Liam has done lots of felt pen drawings of superheroes and put them all over his bedroom walls.

Some things you will find in Liam's foster home

* Lots of cupboards and boxes where you can put toys when you've finished playing with them.
* Liam's pictures from school stuck on the fridge.
* Fruit in a bowl
* Photos of Liam and all the family.

At both houses there are heaps of shells and pebbles Liam has collected from the seaside when he visits his Gran.

Sharon lets Liam make fruit salad for tea sometimes.

First he wipes 1 apple and 1 pear and chops them up.
Then he peels 2 satsumas and 2 bananas, separating the segments of the satsumas and chopping the bananas.
Next he puts all the fruit in a bowl with some orange juice, and stirs it up.

The hardest part is sharing it out so that everyone has some of the different fruits.

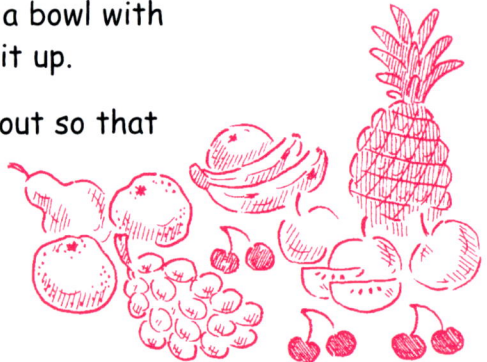

The Little Book of Persona Dolls

Some talking points for younger children

? Liam has lots of friends at his new nursery school. How do you think he felt on the first day?

? Do you ever miss your mum? How do you feel when you see her again?

? Who looks after you when your mum can't be there?

Some talking points for older children

? Why do you think Liam has to be looked after by Sharon and Jim?

? Sometimes the other children ask Liam where his mum is. What could he say?

? One day, some kids teased Liam. They called him 'Titch'. How did Liam feel? What could he do about it?

? It will be Liam's birthday soon. What do you think he would like to eat at his party?

? Once, Liam took Jamie's Spiderman doll. Why do you think he did that? Do you feel like doing that sometimes?

and for the philosophers in your setting!

? Sometimes Liam goes to stay with his mum. When it's time to go back to Sharon and Jim's house, he cries. Why do you think he cries? What could Sharon and Jim do to make him feel better?

Introducing
Annabelle

Annabelle's persona

* Annabelle is five. She has curly brown hair and brown eyes.
* She has an older brother called Oliver who is her best friend and a Mum and Dad.
* Annabelle uses a wheel chair to get about because she cannot walk at all.
* She goes to a special school where there are ramps and wide doorways for her wheelchair to fit through.
* There is also a swimming pool for hydrotherapy.

The Little Book of Persona Dolls

What Annabelle likes, thinks and believes

* Annabelle loves painting and watching Art Attack on TV
* She loves playing dominoes with Oliver. They play on a special table that fixes to her wheelchair. They also play computer games together.
* Annabelle likes going for walks with her family. They go to the woods and the wheels on her wheelchair get really muddy!
* Sometimes they all go to the cinema. Annabelle's favourite film is Toy Story. She has it on video too.
* But best of all, Annabelle enjoys cooking!

The best days of Annabelle's year are:
* The school concert in the summer, when her family come to hear her sing.
* Her birthday, when she helps to make her own birthday cake.
* Springtime, when they all go to see the bluebells in the woods.

What Annabelle wishes

❂ Annabelle wishes that everyone would be kind to each other.

❂ She wishes she could go for a walk in the woods every day.

❂ Annabelle would like to learn to swim. She goes in the school pool every day, and her arms are getting stronger, but her legs still don't work very well.

Some things you will find in Annabelle's home

* Ramps leading to and from her front and back door, so the wheelchair can move easily.
* Special handles by her bed, the bath and toilet for Annabelle to hold on to
* A special computer, with a joystick to help her move the cursor. She likes to use it to play games and draw pictures.
* Oliver and Annabelle have a lot of CD's which they listen to when she gets home from school.
* Annabelle has lots of soft toys - they are everywhere!

All Alone Cake

Annabelle can make this cake all by herself. It tastes delicious! perhaps you would like to try making it.

Use a clean yoghurt pot to measure everything:
<u>What you need</u>:
   * 1 pot of natural yoghurt
   * 3 pots of self-raising flour
   * 2 eggs
   * 2 pots of sugar
   * half a pot of cooking oil.
<u>What you do</u>:
   1.   Mix everything together.
   2.   Oil a round cake tin and pour the mixture in
   3.   Ask a grown-up to put it in a hot oven (180C) for about half an hour.

The Little Book of Persona Dolls

Some talking points for younger children

? Annabelle uses a wheelchair to get about. Do you know anyone who uses a wheelchair?

? Annabelle loves cooking. What can you cook? What is your favourite food?

? Can you swim?

Some talking points for older children

? Annabelle would like an electric wheel-chair. Why do you think she wants one?

? What do you think is the hardest thing for Annabelle to do by herself?

? One day a boy teased Annabelle and said she was stupid because she can't walk. Is that true? How do you think Annabelle felt?

? When Annabelle goes shopping with her mum, it takes ages! Why do you think it takes so long?

? Annabelle has cerebral palsy. How can we find out more about cerebral palsy?

? If Annabelle came to tea at your house, what games could you play together?

? Computer games are good fun. Annabelle likes winning and she sometimes gets cross when she loses. Do you feel like this sometimes? What could you do?

and for the philosophers in your setting!

? How do you think Annabelle feels when people stare at her?

? How do you think she feels when she sees other children running or swimming?

Introducing
Ravinder

Ravinder's persona

* Ravinder is five and a half. His sister, Jasvinder is 11.
* Ravinder is the tallest person in his class (except for Mrs Shah!)
* Ravinder is a Sikh and so are all his family. His mum works in a supermarket and his dad is an engineer. He sometimes works very late at his office.
* He wears his long black hair tied in a knot on the top of his head. He has brown eyes, dark brown skin and a big smile.
* His favourite foods are pickled onion Monster Munch and pakora (vegetables fried in gram flour batter made from chick peas).

What Ravinder likes, thinks and believes

* Ravinder really enjoys watching TV and videos. Sometimes he watches them when his mum and dad are busy in the shop. He doesn't like the scary bits of the films, and he likes cartoons and wildlife films best.
* Ravinder loves insects and minibeasts. He wishes other kids weren't scared of minibeasts. Sometimes they stamp on them!
* Ravinder's whole family are vegetarians because they believe it is wrong to eat meat, fish and eggs.
* All the family go the Gurdwara. The Gurdwara is a big building where Sikhs go to listen to special words and music.
* Their Holy Book is called the Guru Granth Sahib and they look after it with great care.

The best days of Ravinder's year are:
* Divali which comes in the Autumn.
* Baisakhi in the Spring, a festival with a drumming procession.
* The birthday in November of Guru Nanak, the founder of the Sikh faith.

NB. Some Sikh people worship at home instead of the Gurdwara and some cut their hair but they all believe in one God and trying to be better people.

What Ravinder wishes

⊕ Ravinder wishes his mum and dad could meet him from school some days. He misses them when he walks home with his sister Jasvinder, and when they are watching television.

⊕ He wishes his hair would dry quicker after swimming.

⊕ Ravinder wishes he could play one of the drums in the Baisakhi procession. His dad says he will start to teach him how to play the drums when he is seven.

Some things you will find in Ravinder's home

* Ravinder's bug books all over the settee.
* A big TV for watching Asian movies and news.
* A computer in one corner because Ravinder's Mum likes shopping on the Internet.
* A beautiful picture of the Golden Temple in India, which is a very special place for Sikhs.
* Lots of extra big pans in the kitchen for cooking rice and vegetable curries for the whole family and their friends.
* A Khanda: the Sikh symbol which has a circle for the one God all around and swords which mean 'defend the truth'
* Some tablas – Indian drums, that his Dad plays.
* A calendar with pictures of the 10 Gurus (Sikh teachers).

Here's a recipe for roti. They look like pancakes. Ravinder and Jaswinder make them every day for dinner.

What you need:

* a non stick frying pan
* 1 cup of plain flour
* warm water
* 1 tablespoon of cooking oil
* a rolling pin

What you do:

1. Mix the flour and oil together, and add water till you have a thick dough that you can roll out. Let the dough rest for a few minutes.
2. Take pieces of dough about the size of a small apple.
3. Roll into a ball, flatten the ball into a thin circle with the rolling pin.
4. Cook your roti on a non stick frying pan (adult only!).
5. Eat warm with yogurt or butter.

The Little Book of Persona Dolls

Some talking points for younger children

? Have you ever been in a parade? What did you feel like?

? At the weekends Ravinder helps his Dad in the shop by putting the newspapers outside for people to buy. Do you do special things for your Mum or Dad?

Some talking points for older children

? When it is the spring festival of Bhaisakhi some Sikhs from his Gurdwara parade throughout the city with a new flag for the Gurdwara. All the traffic stops and everyone watches them go by. How do you think Ravinder feels when he sees this?

? Sometimes people laugh at Ravinder when his Grandad comes to fetch him from school because his grandad is old and can't speak English. What do you think Ravinder should do about that?

? Ravinder has very dark brown skin and looks different from white people. Why do you think he has dark brown skin?

? When he goes to the Gurdwara with his Mum and Dad he has to concentrate hard to understand the Punjabi words. What do you think it must be like to speak and think in 2 languages? Can you speak two languages?

and for the philosophers in your setting!

? In Sikhism boys and girls, men and women are all equal. Is this fair?

Introducing
Mary-Anne

Mary-Anne's persona

* Mary-Anne is just five. She has long brown hair in plaits, grey eyes and pink cheeks.

* She is an English Gypsy and she lives in a trailer (sometimes called a caravan) with her dad, her mum and her twin baby brothers Kenny and Kim.

* Her favourite food is anything her mum cooks, specially stew.

* Mary-Anne's dad does odd jobs for people, like gardening or block paving. In the autumn he does potato picking.

What Mary-Anne likes, thinks and believes

* Mary-Anne loves being out of doors. She has lots of adventures wherever her dad parks the trailer.
* She likes making new friends. She has already been to lots of different schools.
* Mary-Anne enjoys living in a trailer. She likes all her family close to her, and it's fun travelling around and stopping at different places
* Mary-Anne likes making things from bits and pieces of junk she finds as she travels. She has her own little tool box that her dad gave her. it has screwdrivers and a hammer in it.

The best days of Mary-Anne's year are:
* Going to the horse fair every year and looking at the ponies.
* The first day of potato picking in Norfolk, where they stay on a farm and Mary-Anne can play with the farmer's children.
* Days when she helps her dad to fix the engine of their pickup truck.

What Mary-Anne wishes

❀ Mary-Anne wishes that everyone she meets would smile at her when she smiles at them.

❀ Sometimes she wishes she was older and could work with her dad when he is gardening.

❀ Mary-Anne wishes her baby brothers would stop wriggling about in the night. they sleep in the same bed as her and they keep waking her up!

Some things you will find in Mary-Anne's home

* Her mum and dad collect plates with dogs and cats on. They have to wrap them in towels every time they move so they don't get broken.
* Her dad's accordion. He plays it when they have visitors.
* A stainless steel churn and some plastic water carriers. There is no tap in the trailer so they have to fetch all their water from someone else's tap.
* Some very fancy cushions that Mary-Anne's Grandmother made a long time ago.
* A really lacy tablecloth on the table. Mary-Anne always puts her fingers in the holes and gets told off!
* A tin with Mary-Anne's special collection of nuts and bolts and screws and washers. She uses them to make patterns and pictures.
* Lots of paper and silk flowers in vases. Mary-Anne's mum makes them.

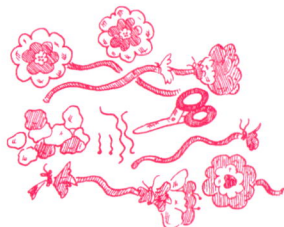

Mary-Anne uses her collection of bits to make pictures and patterns. You could try one too.

What you need:
* a collection of screws, washers, nails, nuts, bolts, etc.
* paper, card squares, small trays, or damp sand to make the patterns on
* paint if you want to make prints

What you do:
Use the objects to make patterns on the paper, prints in the sand or prints with paint. See if you can make a picture of Mary-Anne's trailer and pickup.

The Little Book of Persona Dolls

Some talking points for younger children

? Would you like to live in a trailer and move around from place to place?

? Have you slept in a caravan on holiday?

? Do you like meeting new children and making friends?

Some talking points for older children

? Mary-Anne goes for walks and adventures in the fields round her trailer. Have you ever had an outdoor adventure?

? One day a girl teased Mary-Anne. She said Mary-Anne didn't have a proper home and that her trailer was dirty. This isn't true. How do you think Mary-Anne felt? What could she do?

? Do you collect things? What do you collect?

? Mary-Anne loves her baby brothers very much, but they do keep her awake. What could she do?

? Mary-Anne has to work very hard to make sure she doesn't forget what she does at school. Sometimes she does home work with her mum. Do you do work at home sometimes?

? Some of the people in the town don't want Mary-Anne and her family to stay. How do you think Mary-Anne feels about that?

and for the philosophers in your setting!

? One day Mary-Anne went to play in the Lego. Some boys said 'You can't play here, you're a girl. Girls don't play with Lego.' How did she feel? What do you think? Are some toys just for boys and some toys just for girls?

Introducing
Joseph

Joseph's persona

* Joseph is six. He has brown hair and brown eyes.
* He can speak two languages, Hebrew and English. Joseph and his family are Jewish.
* He has a sister called Sarah Leah, his mum is a nurse and his dad works part time in an electrical shop in town.
* Joseph has a puppy called Spot. He takes Spot for walks every day. His dad comes with Sarah Leah in the push chair.
* Joseph's favourite food is chicken and latke (potato cakes).

What Joseph likes, thinks and believes

* Joseph loves taking his dog for walks. He can have a good chat to his dad about all sorts of things as they walk along.
* He also likes reading to his mum while she is feeding Sarah Leah.
* Joseph and his family go to the synagogue each week to pray to God. They go there every Shabbat (Saturday)
* On Friday evenings, the family has a special meal of fish or chicken with plaited bread called Challah. They say special blessings over the food before they eat it.
* When he is praying, Joseph wears a small round hat called a kippah.
* The Jewish holy book is called the Torah, and it is written in a language called Hebrew.

The best days of Joseph's year are:
* Purim, a lively Spring festival.
* Sukkot - a harvest festival.
* Hannukah, a winter festival of light.

Some Jewish people eat specially prepared food called kosher food.

What Joseph wishes

❁ Joseph wishes that everyone would be kind to animals.

❁ He wishes that his mum didn't have to work shifts. Sometimes he doesn't see her at bedtime, because she is working late.

❁ Joseph would like to take Spot to school to show his friends. His dad says they can't because he takes Joseph to school and then takes Sarah Leah to Grandma's on his way to work. He would have to take Spot to work too!

Some things you will find in Joseph's home

* Candles and candlesticks which are very important for Jewish people.
* Books written in hebrew and books written in English.
* Some special Jewish spinning tops called dreidel.
* Pictures of the Holy Land. Joseph's mum and dad would really like to go there.
* Photos of Joseph's cousins, who live in America. He would like to go there!
* A new basket for Spot. He should in it but he would much rather sleep on the settee or on Joseph's bed!
* Sometimes the house gets very untidy because Joseph's dad doesn't like housework!

Here is a dreidel pattern. You could make your own dreidel to play a Jewish game.

What you need:
* a square piece of card
* some raisins or counters   * a short stick or pencil

What you do:

1. Copy or trace the square, decorate it with Hebrew letters, and write the words on the edges.

2. Ask a grown up to help you push the stick or pencil through the middle of the square.

3. Take 10 raisins or counters each.

4. Spin the top, and when it stops, do what it says on the side touching the table.

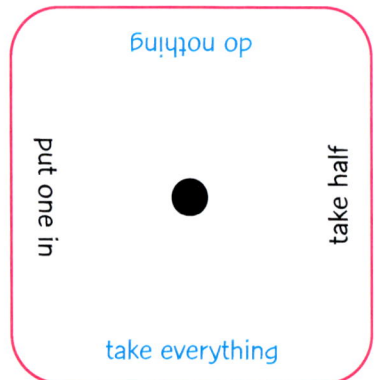

do nothing

put one in

take half

take everything

Some talking points for younger children

? Does your dad sometimes look after you? What do you do with your dad?

? Have you ever taken a dog for a walk? What did you have to do?

? Have you got a pet? How do you take care of it?

Some talking points for older children

? In the spring, at Succoth, Joseph and his family make a shelter in the garden and decorate it with leaves and flowers. What do you do with your family?

? When Joseph is twelve, he will have a special ceremony and party called Bar Mitzvah. Will you have a special celebration when you grow up? How could you find out?

? When Joseph's family get together, his grandparents come and make sure he is learning about Jewish things. What do your relatives ask you when they come to see you? What do you talk about?

? Once, Joseph's friends saw him going to the synagogue wearing his special kippah, and they laughed at him. How do you think he felt? What could he do?

and for the philosophers in your setting!

? Joseph's friend Lily goes to Sunday School at her church. One day Joseph said his synagogue was better than Lily's. How do you think Lily felt? What could she say?

The Little Book of Persona Dolls

Introducing
Nathan

Nathan's persona

* Nathan is just five. He has short brown hair and grey eyes. He is tall and strong. He loves being outside where he can run and make a noise.
* Nathan has four older brothers and they all like beans on toast!
* He has a mum and dad. Nathan's dad is in prison at the moment, so he is not at home.
* They all live in a house with three bedrooms, so Nathan has to share a room with two of his brothers.
* Nathan's mum loves her boys, but she sometimes gets very tired.

What Nathan likes, thinks and believes

* Nathan really likes playing outside with his brothers. They all play football, but sometimes his brothers get the ball and won't let him play. They call him 'Baby' and they run past him and push him over. This makes Nathan really cross!
* Nathan loves playing outside at school too. he never wants to come in! He likes the red bike best and sometimes gets cross with other children when they get it first.
* He likes being strong and tall and he thinks this makes him the best person in his class! Sometimes the other children are a bit scared of him.
* Nathan likes helping, specially when it means carrying things or moving something heavy.
* He likes drawing, specially cars, trucks and diggers, but he doesn't like writing very much.

The best days of Nathan's year are:
* When they go to visit his dad in the prison. His his mum always looks happy on those days.
* Sometimes his brothers are all out and Nathan has a cuddle under a blanket on the settee with his mum.
* All their birthdays, because they go to Burger King.

What Nathan wishes

✿ Nathan wishes his dad would come home soon. He misses him very much.

✿ Some days he wishes he could stay at home with his mum.

✿ He wishes the other children wanted to play his games.

Some things you will find in Nathan's home

* Lots of muddy shoes by the door, and coats and school bags hanging on the end of the stairs.
* Bikes and trikes in the garden. Some of them are broken.
* Toy cars, trucks, superhero models and their weapons.
* A lot of china cats that Nathan's mum collects. Some of them are a bit chipped because they have been knocked over!
* A big TV set and lots of videos.
* Comics and magazines. His mum likes magazines about pop music and films. His brothers like football comics and magazines and they don't like throwing them away, so they have got lots of them everywhere.
* Sometimes Nathan's house is full of kids because his brothers all bring their friends round.

Nathan likes drawing his toy cars and diggers. His mum helps him to label all the parts and he sends them to his dad at the prison.

Could you make a labelled drawing of one of your toys?

Some talking points for younger children

? Who do you play with after school and at the weekends?

? Have you got a favourite outside toy? How do you feel when someone else want to play with it?

? What is your favourite food? Do you like beans on toast?

Some talking points for older children

? Nathan's mum collects china cats. How do you think she feels when the boys knock them over? What do you think she says? What could the boys do?

? Sometimes Nathan is so busy rushing about, he knocks other children over. How do you think they feel? What could they say to Nathan? What should Nathan do?

? Did your mum or dad ever have to go away for a time? How did you feel? How did you feel when they came back?

? Nathan is big and strong. Sometimes the little kids are scared of him because he shouts and pushes them. What could they do about this?

? Nathan's brothers tease him because he is can't run as fast as they can. He feels awful when this happens. What could you say to him to make him feel better?

? Sometimes Nathan's friends ask him where his dad is, and Nathan gets upset. What do you think he could do to cheer himself up?

and for the philosophers in your setting!

? Nathan's mum often gets very tired. Why do you think this is? What could the boys do about this?

The Little Book of Persona Dolls

Books etc.

Combating Discrimination (persona dolls in action), Babette Brown, Trentham Books. ISBN1 85856 239 2

Kids Like Us (using persona dolls in the classroom), Trisha Whitney, Redleaf Press. ISBN 1 884834 65 5

Children Just Like Me Dorling Kinderesley. ISBN 0 7513 5327 2
and others in this series give positive images in photographs and words of children from a variety of cultures and backgrounds.

Persona Dolls in Action (video) available from Featherstone Education

Suppliers

eduzone
29 Friern Barnet Road, London N11 1NE
tel: 08456 44 55 56   **fax**: 08456 44 55 57
email: eduzone.co.uk   **www**.eduzone.co.uk
a wide range of dolls of all nationalities, soft bodied (like William), rag dolls with removable clothing, vinyl dolls (a wide ethnic range with appropriate clothing)

ASCO
19 Lockwood Way, Leeds LS11 5TH
tel: 0113 270 7070   **fax**: 0113 277 5585
email: tom@binder.tele2.co.uk
a range of dolls including persona dolls, soft bodied with removable clothing (like Nathan), and accessories - wheelchairs, football kit, etc.

NES Arnold
Excelsior Road, Ashby de la Zouch,
Leicestershire LE65 1NG
tel: 0845 120 4525
www.nesarnold.co.uk

Training

www.persona-doll-training.org provides training and a range of resources, including dolls from many cultures.

If you have found this book useful you might also like ...

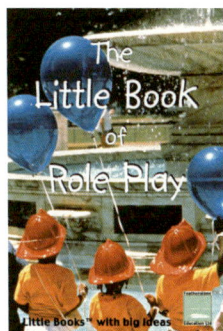

The Little Book of Role Play
LB2
ISBN 1-902233-62-X

The Little Book of Prop Boxes for Role Play
LB6
ISBN 1-902233-63-8

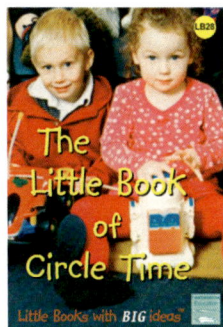

The Little Book of Circle Time
LB28
ISBN 1-904187-94-3

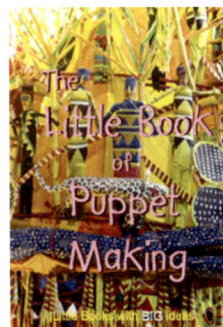

The Little Book of Puppet Making
LB23
ISBN 1-904187-73-0

All available from

Featherstone Education   PO Box 6350

Lutterworth LE17 6ZA

T:0185 888 1212   F:0185 888 1360

on our web site

www.featherstone.uk.com

and from selected
book suppliers

The Little Books Club

Little Books meet the need for exciting and practical activities which are fun to do, address the Early Learning Goals and can be followed in most settings. As one user put it

"When everything else falls apart I know I can reach for a Little Book and things will be fine!"

We publish 10 Little Books a year – one a month except for August and December. **Little Books Club members receive each <u>new</u> Little Book on approval at a reduced price** as soon as it is published.

Examine the book at your leisure. Keep it or return it. You decide.

That's all. No strings. No joining fee. No agreement to buy a set number of books during the year. And you can leave at any time.

Little Books Club members receive -

♥   *each new Little Book on approval as soon as it's published*

♥   *a specially reduced price on that book and on any other Little Books they buy*

♥   *a regular, free newsletter dealing with club news and aspects of Early Years curriculum and practice*

♥   *free postage on anything ordered from our catalogue*

♥   *a discount voucher on joining which can be used to buy from our catalogue*

♥   *at least one other special offer every month*

There's always something in Little Books to help and inspire you!

Phone 0185 888 1212 for details